MEDITERRANEAN COOKBOOK 2021

MANY TASTY AND AFFORDABLE RECIPES

PAULINA DI CARO

Table of Contents

Slow Cooker Meatloaf

Preparation Time : 10 minutes

Cooking Time : 6 hours and 10 minutes

Servings : 8

Difficulty Level : Average

Ingredients:

- 2 pounds Ground bison
- 1 Grated zucchini
- 2 large Eggs
- Olive oil cooking spray as required
- 1 Zucchini, shredded
- ½ cup Parsley, fresh, finely chopped
- ½ cup Parmesan cheese, shredded
- 3 tablespoons Balsamic vinegar
- 4 Garlic cloves, grated
- 2 tablespoons Onion minced
- 1 tablespoon Dried oregano
- ½ teaspoon Ground black pepper
- ½ teaspoon Kosher salt
- For the topping:
- ¼ cup Shredded Mozzarella cheese
- ¼ cup Ketchup without sugar
- ¼ cup Freshly chopped parsley

Directions:

Stripe line the inside of a six-quart slow cooker with aluminum foil. Spray non-stick cooking oil over it.

In a large bowl combine ground bison or extra lean ground sirloin, zucchini, eggs, parsley, balsamic vinegar, garlic, dried oregano, sea or kosher salt, minced dry onion, and ground black pepper.

Situate this mixture into the slow cooker and form an oblong shaped loaf. Cover the cooker, set on a low heat and cook for 6 hours. After cooking, open the cooker and spread ketchup all over the meatloaf.

Now, place the cheese above the ketchup as a new layer and close the slow cooker. Let the meatloaf sit on these two layers for about 10 minutes or until the cheese starts to melt. Garnish with fresh parsley, and shredded Mozzarella cheese.

Nutrition (for 100g): 320 Calories 2g Fat 4g Carbohydrates 26g Protein 681mg Sodium

Slow Cooker Mediterranean Beef Hoagies

Preparation Time : 10 minutes

Cooking Time : 13 hours

Servings : 6

Difficulty Level : Average

Ingredients:

- 3 pounds Beef top round roast fatless
- ½ teaspoon Onion powder
- ½ teaspoon Black pepper
- 3 cups Low sodium beef broth
- 4 teaspoons Salad dressing mix
- 1 Bay leaf
- 1 tablespoon Garlic, minced
- 2 Red bell peppers, thin strips cut
- 16 ounces Pepperoncino
- 8 slices Sargento Provolone, thin
- 2 ounces Gluten-free bread
- ½ teaspoon salt
- For seasoning:
- 1½ tablespoon Onion powder
- 1½ tablespoon Garlic powder
- 2 tablespoon Dried parsley
- 1 tablespoon stevia
- ½ teaspoon Dried thyme

- 1 tablespoon Dried oregano
- 2 tablespoons Black pepper
- 1 tablespoon Salt
- 6 Cheese slices

Directions:

Dry the roast with a paper towel. Combine black pepper, onion powder and salt in a small bowl and rub the mixture over the roast. Place the seasoned roast into a slow cooker.

Add broth, salad dressing mix, bay leaf, and garlic to the slow cooker. Combine it gently. Close and set to low cooking for 12 hours. After cooking, remove the bay leaf.

Take out the cooked beef and shred the beef meet. Put back the shredded beef and add bell peppers and. Add bell peppers and pepperoncino into the slow cooker. Cover the cooker and low cook for 1 hour. Before serving, top each of the bread with 3 ounces of the meat mixture. Top it with a cheese slice. The liquid gravy can be used as a dip.

Nutrition (for 100g): 442 Calories 11.5g Fat 37g Carbohydrates 49g Protein 735mg Sodium

Mediterranean Pork Roast

Preparation Time : 10 minutes

Cooking Time : 8 hours and 10 minutes

Servings : 6

Difficulty Level : Average

Ingredients:

- 2 tablespoons Olive oil
- 2 pounds Pork roast
- ½ teaspoon Paprika
- ¾ cup Chicken broth
- 2 teaspoons Dried sage
- ½ tablespoon Garlic minced
- ¼ teaspoon Dried marjoram
- ¼ teaspoon Dried Rosemary
- 1 teaspoon Oregano
- ¼ teaspoon Dried thyme
- 1 teaspoon Basil
- ¼ teaspoon Kosher salt

Directions:

In a small bowl mix broth, oil, salt, and spices. In a skillet pour olive oil and bring to medium-high heat. Put the pork into it and roast until all sides become brown.

Take out the pork after cooking and poke the roast all over with a knife. Place the poked pork roast into a 6-quart crock pot. Now, pour the small bowl mixture liquid all over the roast.

Seal crock pot and cook on low for 8 hours. After cooking, remove it from the crock pot on to a cutting board and shred into pieces. Afterward, add the shredded pork back into the crockpot. Simmer it another 10 minutes. Serve along with feta cheese, pita bread, and tomatoes.

Nutrition (for 100g): 361 Calories 10.4g Fat 0.7g Carbohydrates 43.8g Protein 980mg Sodium

Beef Pizza

Preparation Time : 20 minutes

Cooking Time : 50 minutes

Servings : 10

Difficulty Level : Difficult

Ingredients:

- <u>For Crust:</u>
- 3 cups all-purpose flour
- 1 tablespoon sugar
- 2¼ teaspoons active dry yeast
- 1 teaspoon salt
- 2 tablespoons olive oil
- 1 cup warm water
- <u>For Topping:</u>
- 1-pound ground beef
- 1 medium onion, chopped
- 2 tablespoons tomato paste
- 1 tablespoon ground cumin
- Salt and ground black pepper, as required
- ¼ cup water
- 1 cup fresh spinach, chopped
- 8 ounces artichoke hearts, quartered
- 4 ounces fresh mushrooms, sliced

- 2 tomatoes, chopped
- 4 ounces feta cheese, crumbled

Directions:

For crust:

Mix the flour, sugar, yeast and salt with a stand mixer, using the dough hook. Add 2 tablespoons of the oil and warm water and knead until a smooth and elastic dough is formed.

Make a ball of the dough and set aside for about 15 minutes.

Situate the dough onto a lightly floured surface and roll into a circle. Situate the dough into a lightly, greased round pizza pan and gently, press to fit. Set aside for about 10-15 minutes. Coat the crust with some oil. Preheat the oven to 400 degrees F.

For topping:

Fry beef in a nonstick skillet over medium-high heat for about 4-5 minutes. Mix in the onion and cook for about 5 minutes, stirring frequently. Add the tomato paste, cumin, salt, black pepper and water and stir to combine.

Set the heat to medium and cook for about 5-10 minutes. Remove from the heat and set aside. Place the beef mixture over the pizza crust and top with the spinach, followed by the artichokes, mushrooms, tomatoes, and Feta cheese.

Bake until the cheese is melted. Remove from the oven and set aside for about 3-5 minutes before slicing. Cut into desired sized slices and serve.

Nutrition (for 100g): 309 Calories 8.7g Fat 3.7g Carbohydrates 3.3g Protein 732mg Sodium

Beef & Bulgur Meatballs

Preparation Time : 20 minutes

Cooking Time : 28 minutes

Servings : 6

Difficulty Level : Average

Ingredients:

- ¾ cup uncooked bulgur
- 1-pound ground beef
- ¼ cup shallots, minced
- ¼ cup fresh parsley, minced
- ½ teaspoon ground allspice
- ½ teaspoon ground cumin
- ½ teaspoon ground cinnamon
- ¼ teaspoon red pepper flakes, crushed
- Salt, as required
- 1 tablespoon olive oil

Directions:

In a large bowl of the cold water, soak the bulgur for about 30 minutes. Drain the bulgur well and then, squeeze with your hands to remove the excess water. In a food processor, add the bulgur, beef, shallot, parsley, spices, salt, and pulse until a smooth mixture is formed.

Situate the mixture into a bowl and refrigerate, covered for about 30 minutes. Remove from the refrigerator and make equal sized balls from the beef mixture. In a large nonstick skillet, heat the oil over medium-high heat and cook the meatballs in 2 batches for about 13-14 minutes, flipping frequently. Serve warm.

Nutrition (for 100g): 228 Calories 7.4g Fat 0.1g Carbohydrates 3.5g Protein 766mg Sodium

Tasty Beef and Broccoli

Preparation Time : 10 minutes

Cooking Time : 15 minutes

Servings : 4

Difficulty Level : Easy

Ingredients:

- 1 and ½ lbs. flanks steak
- 1 tbsp. olive oil
- 1 tbsp. tamari sauce
- 1 cup beef stock
- 1-pound broccoli, florets separated

Directions:

Combine steak strips with oil and tamari, toss and set aside for 10 minutes. Select your instant pot on sauté mode, place beef strips and brown them for 4 minutes on each side. Stir in stock, cover the pot again and cook on high for 8 minutes. Stir in broccoli, cover and cook on high for 4 minutes more. Portion everything between plates and serve. Enjoy!

Nutrition (for 100g): 312 Calories 5g Fat 20g Carbohydrates 4g Protein 694mg Sodium

Beef Corn Chili

Preparation Time : 8-10 minutes

Cooking Time : 30 minutes

Servings : 8

Difficulty Level : Average

Ingredients:

- 2 small onions, chopped (finely)
- ¼ cup canned corn
- 1 tablespoon oil
- 10 ounces lean ground beef
- 2 small chili peppers, diced

Directions:

Turn on the instant pot. Click "SAUTE". Pour the oil then stir in the onions, chili pepper, and beef; cook until turn translucent and softened. Pour the 3 cups water in the Cooking pot; mix well.

Seal the lid. Select "MEAT/STEW". Adjust the timer to 20 minutes. Allow to cook until the timer turns to zero.

Click "CANCEL" then "NPR" for natural release pressure for about 8-10 minutes. Open then place the dish in serving plates. Serve.

Nutrition (for 100g): 94 Calories 5g Fat 2g Carbohydrates 7g Protein 477mg Sodium

Balsamic Beef Dish

Preparation Time : 5 minutes

Cooking Time : 55 minutes

Servings : 8

Difficulty Level : Average

Ingredients:

- 3 pounds chuck roast
- 3 cloves garlic, thinly sliced
- 1 tablespoon oil
- 1 teaspoon flavored vinegar
- ½ teaspoon pepper
- ½ teaspoon rosemary
- 1 tablespoon butter
- ½ teaspoon thyme
- ¼ cup balsamic vinegar
- 1 cup beef broth

Directions:

Slice the slits in the roast and stuff in garlic slices all over. Combine flavored vinegar, rosemary, pepper, thyme and rub the mixture over the roast. Select the pot on sauté mode and mix in oil, allow the oil to heat up. Cook both side of the roast.

Take it out and set aside. Stir in butter, broth, balsamic vinegar and deglaze the pot. Return the roast and close the lid, then cook on HIGH pressure for 40 minutes.

Perform a quick release. Serve!

Nutrition (for 100g): 393 Calories 15g Fat 25g Carbohydrates 37g Protein 870mg Sodium

Soy Sauce Beef Roast

Preparation Time : 8 minutes

Cooking Time : 35 minutes

Servings : 2-3

Difficulty Level : Average

Ingredients:

- ½ teaspoon beef bouillon
- 1 ½ teaspoon rosemary
- ½ teaspoon minced garlic
- 2 pounds roast beef
- 1/3 cup soy sauce

Directions:

Combine the soy sauce, bouillon, rosemary, and garlic together in a mixing bowl.

Turn on your instant pot. Place the roast, and pour enough water to cover the roast; gently stir to mix well. Seal it tight.

Click "MEAT/STEW" Cooking function; set pressure level to "HIGH" and set the Cooking time to 35 minutes. Let the pressure to build to cook the ingredients. Once done, click "CANCEL" setting then click "NPR" Cooking function to release the pressure naturally.

Gradually open the lid, and shred the meat. Mix in the shredded meat back in the potting mix and stir well. Transfer in serving containers. Serve warm.

Nutrition (for 100g): 423 Calories 14g Fat 12g Carbohydrates 21g Protein 884mg Sodium

Rosemary Beef Chuck Roast

Preparation Time : 5 minutes

Cooking Time : 45 minutes

Servings : 5-6

Difficulty Level : Average

Ingredients:

- 3 pounds chuck beef roast
- 3 garlic cloves
- ¼ cup balsamic vinegar
- 1 sprig fresh rosemary
- 1 sprig fresh thyme
- 1 cup of water
- 1 tablespoon vegetable oil
- Salt and pepper to taste

Directions:

Chop slices in the beef roast and place the garlic cloves in them. Rub the roast with the herbs, black pepper, and salt. Preheat your instant pot using the sauté setting and pour the oil. When warmed, mix in the beef roast and stir-cook until browned on all sides. Add the remaining ingredients; stir gently.

Seal tight and cook on high for 40 minutes using manual setting. Allow the pressure release naturally, about 10 minutes. Uncover and put the beef roast the serving plates, slice and serve.

Nutrition (for 100g): 542 Calories 11.2g Fat 8.7g Carbohydrates 55.2g Protein 710mg Sodium

Pork Chops and Tomato Sauce

Preparation Time : 10 minutes

Cooking Time : 20 minutes

Servings : 4

Difficulty Level : Easy

Ingredients:

- 4 pork chops, boneless
- 1 tablespoon soy sauce
- ¼ teaspoon sesame oil
- 1 and ½ cups tomato paste
- 1 yellow onion
- 8 mushrooms, sliced

Directions:

In a bowl, mix pork chops with soy sauce and sesame oil, toss and leave aside for 10 minutes. Set your instant pot on sauté mode, add pork chops and brown them for 5 minutes on each side. Stir in onion, and cook for 1-2 minutes more. Add tomato paste and mushrooms, toss, cover and cook on high for 8-9 minutes. Divide everything between plates and serve. Enjoy!

Nutrition (for 100g): 300 Calories 7g Fat 18g Carbohydrates 4g Protein 801mg Sodium

Chicken with Caper Sauce

Preparation Time : 10 minutes

Cooking Time : 18 minutes

Servings : 5

Difficulty Level : Difficult

Ingredients:

- <u>For Chicken:</u>
- 2 eggs
- Salt and ground black pepper, as required
- 1 cup dry breadcrumbs
- 2 tablespoons olive oil
- 1½ pounds skinless, boneless chicken breast halves, pounded into ¾inch thickness and cut into pieces
- <u>For Capers Sauce:</u>
- 3 tablespoons capers
- ½ cup dry white wine
- 3 tablespoons fresh lemon juice
- Salt and ground black pepper, as required
- 2 tablespoons fresh parsley, chopped

Directions:

For chicken: in a shallow dish, add the eggs, salt and black pepper and beat until well combined. In another shallow dish, place breadcrumbs. Soak the chicken pieces in egg mixture then coat with the breadcrumbs evenly. Shake off the excess breadcrumbs.

Cook the oil over medium heat and cook the chicken pieces for about 5-7 minutes per side or until desired doneness. With a slotted spoon, situate the chicken pieces onto a paper towel lined plate. With a piece of the foil, cover the chicken pieces to keep them warm.

In the same skillet, incorporate all the sauce ingredients except parsley and cook for about 2-3 minutes, stirring continuously. Mix in the parsley and remove from heat. Serve the chicken pieces with the topping of capers sauce.

Nutrition (for 100g): 352 Calories 13.5g Fat 1.9g Carbohydrates 1.2g Protein 741mg Sodium

Turkey Burgers with Mango Salsa

Preparation Time : 15 minutes

Cooking Time : 10 minutes

Servings : 6

Difficulty Level : Easy

Ingredients:

- 1½ pounds ground turkey breast
- 1 teaspoon sea salt, divided
- ¼ teaspoon freshly ground black pepper
- 2 tablespoons extra-virgin olive oil
- 2 mangos, peeled, pitted, and cubed
- ½ red onion, finely chopped
- Juice of 1 lime
- 1 garlic clove, minced
- ½ jalapeño pepper, seeded and finely minced
- 2 tablespoons chopped fresh cilantro leaves

Directions:

Form the turkey breast into 4 patties and season with ½ teaspoon of sea salt and the pepper. Cook the olive oil in a nonstick skillet until it shimmers. Add the turkey patties and cook for about 5 minutes per side until browned. While the patties cook, mix the mango, red onion, lime juice, garlic, jalapeño, cilantro, and remaining ½ teaspoon of sea salt in a small bowl. Spoon the salsa over the turkey patties and serve.

Nutrition (for 100g): 384 Calories 3g Fat 27g Carbohydrates 34g Protein 692mg Sodium

Herb-Roasted Turkey Breast

Preparation Time : 15 minutes

Cooking Time : 1½ hours (plus 20 minutes to rest)

Servings : 6

Difficulty Level : Average

Ingredients:

- 2 tablespoons extra-virgin olive oil
- 4 garlic cloves, minced
- Zest of 1 lemon
- 1 tablespoon chopped fresh thyme leaves
- 1 tablespoon chopped fresh rosemary leaves
- 2 tablespoons chopped fresh Italian parsley leaves
- 1 teaspoon ground mustard
- 1 teaspoon sea salt
- ¼ teaspoon freshly ground black pepper
- 1 (6-pound) bone-in, skin-on turkey breast
- 1 cup dry white wine

Directions:

Preheat the oven to 325°F. Combine the olive oil, garlic, lemon zest, thyme, rosemary, parsley, mustard, sea salt, and pepper. Brush the herb mixture evenly over the surface of the turkey breast, and loosen the skin and rub underneath as well. Situate the turkey breast in a roasting pan on a rack, skin-side up.

Pour the wine in the pan. Roast for 1 to 1½ hours until the turkey reaches an internal temperature of 165 degrees F. Pull out from the oven and set separately for 20 minutes, tented with aluminum foil to keep it warm, before carving.

Nutrition (for 100g): 392 Calories 1g Fat 2g Carbohydrates 84g Protein 741mg Sodium

Chicken Sausage and Peppers

Preparation Time : 10 minutes

Cooking Time : 20 minutes

Servings : 6

Difficulty Level : Average

Ingredients:

- 2 tablespoons extra-virgin olive oil
- 6 Italian chicken sausage links
- 1 onion
- 1 red bell pepper
- 1 green bell pepper
- 3 garlic cloves, minced
- ½ cup dry white wine
- ½ teaspoon sea salt
- ¼ teaspoon freshly ground black pepper
- Pinch red pepper flakes

Directions:

Cook the olive oil on large skillet until it shimmers. Add the sausages and cook for 5 to 7 minutes, turning occasionally, until browned, and they reach an internal temperature of 165°F. With tongs, remove the sausage from the pan and set aside on a platter, tented with aluminum foil to keep warm.

Return the skillet to the heat and mix in the onion, red bell pepper, and green bell pepper. Cook and stir occasionally, until the vegetables begin to brown. Put in the garlic and cook for 30 seconds, stirring constantly.

Stir in the wine, sea salt, pepper, and red pepper flakes. Pull out and fold in any browned bits from the bottom of the pan. Simmer for about 4 minutes more, stirring, until the liquid reduces by half. Spoon the peppers over the sausages and serve.

Nutrition (for 100g): 173 Calories 1g Fat 6g Carbohydrates 22g Protein 582mg Sodium

Chicken Piccata

Preparation Time : 10 minutes

Cooking Time : 15 minutes

Servings : 6

Difficulty Level : Average

Ingredients:

- ½ cup whole-wheat flour
- ½ teaspoon sea salt
- 1/8 teaspoon freshly ground black pepper
- 1½ pounds chicken breasts, cut into 6 pieces
- 3 tablespoons extra-virgin olive oil
- 1 cup unsalted chicken broth
- ½ cup dry white wine
- Juice of 1 lemon
- Zest of 1 lemon
- ¼ cup capers, drained and rinsed
- ¼ cup chopped fresh parsley leaves

Directions:

In a shallow dish, whisk the flour, sea salt, and pepper. Scour the chicken in the flour and tap off any excess. Cook the olive oil until it shimmers.

Put the chicken and cook for about 4 minutes per side until browned. Pull out the chicken from the pan and set aside, tented with aluminum foil to keep warm.

Situate the skillet back to the heat and stir in the broth, wine, lemon juice, lemon zest, and capers. Use the side of a spoon scoop and fold in any browned bits from the pan's bottom. Simmer until the liquid thickens. Take out the skillet from the heat and take the chicken back to the pan. Turn to coat. Stir in the parsley and serve.

Nutrition (for 100g): 153 Calories 2g Fat 9g Carbohydrates 8g Protein 692mg Sodium

One-Pan Tuscan Chicken

Preparation Time : 10 minutes

Cooking Time : 25 minutes

Servings : 6

Difficulty Level : Difficult

Ingredients:

- ¼ cup extra-virgin olive oil, divided
- 1-pound boneless, skinless chicken breasts, cut into ¾-inch pieces
- 1 onion, chopped
- 1 red bell pepper, chopped
- 3 garlic cloves, minced
- ½ cup dry white wine
- 1 (14-ounce) can crushed tomatoes, undrained
- 1 (14-ounce) can chopped tomatoes, drained
- 1 (14-ounce) can white beans, drained
- 1 tablespoon dried Italian seasoning
- ½ teaspoon sea salt
- 1/8 teaspoon freshly ground black pepper
- 1/8 teaspoon red pepper flakes
- ¼ cup chopped fresh basil leaves

Directions:

Cook 2 tablespoons of olive oil until it shimmers. Mix in the chicken and cook until browned. Remove the chicken from the skillet and set aside on a platter, tented with aluminum foil to keep warm.

Situate the skillet back to the heat and heat up the remaining olive oil. Add the onion and red bell pepper. Cook and stir rarely, until the vegetables are soft. Put the garlic and cook for 30 seconds, stirring constantly.

Stir in the wine, and use the side of the spoon to scoop out any browned bits from the bottom of the pan. Cook for 1 minute, stirring.

Mix in the crushed and chopped tomatoes, white beans, Italian seasoning, sea salt, pepper, and red pepper flakes. Allow to simmer. Cook for 5 minutes, stirring occasionally.

Put the chicken back and any juices that have collected to the skillet. Cook until the chicken is cook through. Take out from the heat and stir in the basil before serving.

Nutrition (for 100g): 271 Calories 8g Fat 29g Carbohydrates 14g Protein 596mg Sodium

Chicken Kapama

Preparation Time : 10 minutes

Cooking Time : 2 hours

Servings : 4

Difficulty Level : Average

Ingredients:

- 1 (32-ounce) can chopped tomatoes, drained
- ¼ cup dry white wine
- 2 tablespoons tomato paste
- 3 tablespoons extra-virgin olive oil
- ¼ teaspoon red pepper flakes
- 1 teaspoon ground allspice
- ½ teaspoon dried oregano
- 2 whole cloves
- 1 cinnamon stick
- ½ teaspoon sea salt
- 1/8 teaspoon freshly ground black pepper
- 4 boneless, skinless chicken breast halves

Directions:

Mix the tomatoes, wine, tomato paste, olive oil, red pepper flakes, allspice, oregano, cloves, cinnamon stick, sea salt, and pepper in large pot. Bring to a simmer, stirring occasionally. Allow to simmer for 30 minutes, stirring occasionally. Remove and discard the whole cloves and cinnamon stick from the sauce and let the sauce cool.

Preheat the oven to 350°F. Situate the chicken in a 9-by-13-inch baking dish. Pour the sauce over the chicken and cover the pan with aluminum foil. Continue baking until it reaches 165°F internal temperature.

Nutrition (for 100g): 220 Calories 3g Fat 11g Carbohydrates 8g Protein 923mg Sodium

Spinach and Feta–Stuffed Chicken Breasts

Preparation Time : 10 minutes

Cooking Time : 45 minutes

Servings : 4

Difficulty Level : Average

Ingredients:

- 2 tablespoons extra-virgin olive oil
- 1-pound fresh baby spinach
- 3 garlic cloves, minced
- Zest of 1 lemon
- ½ teaspoon sea salt
- 1/8 teaspoon freshly ground black pepper
- ½ cup crumbled feta cheese
- 4 boneless, skinless chicken breasts

Directions:

Preheat the oven to 350°F. Cook the olive oil over medium heat until it shimmers. Add the spinach. Continue cooking and stirring, until wilted.

Stir in the garlic, lemon zest, sea salt, and pepper. Cook for 30 seconds, stirring constantly. Cool slightly and mix in the cheese.

Spread the spinach and cheese mixture in an even layer over the chicken pieces and roll the breast around the filling. Hold closed with toothpicks or butcher's twine. Place the breasts in a 9-by-13-

inch baking dish and bake for 30 to 40 minutes, or until the chicken have an internal temperature of 165°F. Take out from the oven and set aside for 5 minutes before slicing and serving.

Nutrition (for 100g): 263 Calories 3g Fat 7g Carbohydrates 17g Protein 639mg Sodium

Rosemary Baked Chicken Drumsticks

Preparation Time : 5 minutes

Cooking Time : 1 hour

Servings : 6

Difficulty Level : Easy

Ingredients:

- 2 tablespoons chopped fresh rosemary leaves
- 1 teaspoon garlic powder
- ½ teaspoon sea salt
- 1/8 teaspoon freshly ground black pepper
- Zest of 1 lemon
- 12 chicken drumsticks

Directions:

Preheat the oven to 350°F. Mix the rosemary, garlic powder, sea salt, pepper, and lemon zest.

Situate the drumsticks in a 9-by-13-inch baking dish and sprinkle with the rosemary mixture. Bake until the chicken reaches an internal temperature of 165°F.

Nutrition (for 100g): 163 Calories 1g Fat 2g Carbohydrates 26g Protein 633mg Sodium

Chicken with Onions, Potatoes, Figs, and Carrots

Preparation Time : 5 minutes

Cooking Time : 45 minutes

Servings : 4

Difficulty Level : Average

Ingredients:

- 2 cups fingerling potatoes, halved
- 4 fresh figs, quartered
- 2 carrots, julienned
- 2 tablespoons extra-virgin olive oil
- 1 teaspoon sea salt, divided
- ¼ teaspoon freshly ground black pepper
- 4 chicken leg-thigh quarters
- 2 tablespoons chopped fresh parsley leaves

Directions:

Preheat the oven to 425°F. In a small bowl, toss the potatoes, figs, and carrots with the olive oil, ½ teaspoon of sea salt, and the pepper. Spread in a 9-by-13-inch baking dish.

Season the chicken with the rest of t sea salt. Place it on top of the vegetables. Bake until the vegetables are soft and the chicken reaches an internal temperature of 165°F. Sprinkle with the parsley and serve.

Nutrition (for 100g): 429 Calories 4g Fat 27g Carbohydrates 52g Protein 581mg Sodium

Chicken Gyros with Tzatziki

Preparation Time : 15 minutes

Cooking Time : 1 hours and 20 minutes

Servings : 6

Difficulty Level : Average

Ingredients:

- 1-pound ground chicken breast
- 1 onion, grated with excess water wrung out
- 2 tablespoons dried rosemary
- 1 tablespoon dried marjoram
- 6 garlic cloves, minced
- ½ teaspoon sea salt
- ¼ teaspoon freshly ground black pepper
- Tzatziki Sauce

Directions:

Preheat the oven to 350°F. Mix the chicken, onion, rosemary, marjoram, garlic, sea salt, and pepper using food processor. Blend until the mixture forms a paste. Alternatively, mix these ingredients in a bowl until well combined (see preparation tip).

Press the mixture into a loaf pan. Bake until it reaches 165 degrees internal temperature. Take out from the oven and let rest for 20 minutes before slicing.

Slice the gyro and spoon the tzatziki sauce over the top.

Nutrition (for 100g): 289 Calories 1g Fat 20g Carbohydrates 50g Protein 622mg Sodium

Moussaka

Preparation Time : 10 minutes

Cooking Time : 45 minutes

Servings : 8

Difficulty Level : Difficult

Ingredients:

- 5 tablespoons extra-virgin olive oil, divided
- 1 eggplant, sliced (unpeeled)
- 1 onion, chopped
- 1 green bell pepper, seeded and chopped
- 1-pound ground turkey
- 3 garlic cloves, minced
- 2 tablespoons tomato paste
- 1 (14-ounce) can chopped tomatoes, drained
- 1 tablespoon Italian seasoning
- 2 teaspoons Worcestershire sauce
- 1 teaspoon dried oregano
- ½ teaspoon ground cinnamon
- 1 cup unsweetened nonfat plain Greek yogurt
- 1 egg, beaten
- ¼ teaspoon freshly ground black pepper
- ¼ teaspoon ground nutmeg
- ¼ cup grated Parmesan cheese
- 2 tablespoons chopped fresh parsley leaves

Directions:

Preheat the oven to 400°F. Cook 3 tablespoons of olive oil until it shimmers. Add the eggplant slices and brown for 3 to 4 minutes per side. Transfer to paper towels to drain.

Return the skillet to the heat and pour the remaining 2 tablespoons of olive oil. Add the onion and green bell pepper. Continue cooking until the vegetables are soft. Remove from the pan and set aside.

Pull out the skillet to the heat and stir in the turkey. Cook for about 5 minutes, crumbling with a spoon, until browned. Stir in the garlic and cook for 30 seconds, stirring constantly.

Stir in the tomato paste, tomatoes, Italian seasoning, Worcestershire sauce, oregano, and cinnamon. Place the onion and bell pepper back to the pan. Cook for 5 minutes, stirring. Combine the yogurt, egg, pepper, nutmeg, and cheese.

Arrange half of the meat mixture in a 9-by-13-inch baking dish. Layer with half the eggplant. Add the remaining meat mixture and the remaining eggplant. Spread with the yogurt mixture. Bake until golden brown. Garnish with the parsley and serve.

Nutrition (for 100g): 338 Calories 5g Fat 16g Carbohydrates 28g Protein 569mg Sodium

Dijon and Herb Pork Tenderloin

Preparation Time : 10 minutes

Cooking Time : 30 minutes

Servings : 6

Difficulty Level : Average

Ingredients:

- ½ cup fresh Italian parsley leaves, chopped
- 3 tablespoons fresh rosemary leaves, chopped
- 3 tablespoons fresh thyme leaves, chopped
- 3 tablespoons Dijon mustard
- 1 tablespoon extra-virgin olive oil
- 4 garlic cloves, minced
- ½ teaspoon sea salt
- ¼ teaspoon freshly ground black pepper
- 1 (1½-pound) pork tenderloin

Directions:

Preheat the oven to 400°F. Blend the parsley, rosemary, thyme, mustard, olive oil, garlic, sea salt, and pepper. Process for about 30 seconds until smooth. Spread the mixture evenly over the pork and place it on a rimmed baking sheet.

Bake until the meat reaches an internal temperature of 140°F. Pull out from the oven and set aside for 10 minutes before slicing and serving.

Nutrition (for 100g): 393 Calories 3g Fat 5g Carbohydrates 74g Protein 697mg Sodium

Steak with Red Wine–Mushroom Sauce

Preparation Time : minutes plus 8 hours to marinate

Cooking Time : 20 minutes

Servings : 4

Difficulty Level : Difficult

Ingredients:

- <u>For the Marinade and Steak</u>
- 1 cup dry red wine
- 3 garlic cloves, minced
- 2 tablespoons extra-virgin olive oil
- 1 tablespoon low-sodium soy sauce
- 1 tablespoon dried thyme
- 1 teaspoon Dijon mustard
- 2 tablespoons extra-virgin olive oil
- 1 to 1½ pounds skirt steak, flat iron steak, or tri-tip steak
- <u>For the Mushroom Sauce</u>
- 2 tablespoons extra-virgin olive oil
- 1-pound cremini mushrooms, quartered
- ½ teaspoon sea salt
- 1 teaspoon dried thyme
- 1/8 teaspoon freshly ground black pepper
- 2 garlic cloves, minced
- 1 cup dry red wine

Directions:

To Make the Marinade and Steak

In a small bowl, whisk the wine, garlic, olive oil, soy sauce, thyme, and mustard. Pour into a resealable bag and add the steak. Refrigerate the steak to marinate for 4 to 8 hours. Remove the steak from the marinade and pat it dry with paper towels.

Cook the olive oil in large pan until it shimmers.

Situate the steak and cook for about 4 minutes per side until deeply browned on each side and the steak reaches an internal temperature of 140°F. Remove the steak from the skillet and put it on a plate tented with aluminum foil to keep warm, while you prepare the mushroom sauce.

When the mushroom sauce is ready, slice the steak against the grain into ½-inch-thick slices.

To Make the Mushroom Sauce

Cook oil in the same skillet over medium-high heat. Add the mushrooms, sea salt, thyme, and pepper. Cook for about 6 minutes, stirring very infrequently, until the mushrooms are browned.

Sauté the garlic. Mix in the wine, and use the side of a wooden spoon to scoop out any browned bits from the bottom of the skillet. Cook until the liquid reduces by half. Serve the mushrooms spooned over the steak.

Nutrition (for 100g): 405 Calories 5g Fat 7g Carbohydrates 33g Protein 842mg Sodium

Greek Meatballs

Preparation Time : 20 minutes

Cooking Time : 25 minutes

Servings : 4

Difficulty Level : Average

Ingredients:

- 2 whole-wheat bread slices
- 1¼ pounds ground turkey
- 1 egg
- ¼ cup seasoned whole-wheat bread crumbs
- 3 garlic cloves, minced
- ¼ red onion, grated
- ¼ cup chopped fresh Italian parsley leaves
- 2 tablespoons chopped fresh mint leaves
- 2 tablespoons chopped fresh oregano leaves
- ½ teaspoon sea salt
- ¼ teaspoon freshly ground black pepper

Directions:

Preheat the oven to 350°F. Situate parchment paper or aluminum foil onto the baking sheet. Run the bread under water to wet it, and squeeze out any excess. Shred wet bread into small pieces and place it in a medium bowl.

Add the turkey, egg, bread crumbs, garlic, red onion, parsley, mint, oregano, sea salt, and pepper. Mix well. Form the mixture into ¼-cup-size balls. Place the meatballs on the prepared sheet and bake for about 25 minutes, or until the internal temperature reaches 165°F.

Nutrition (for 100g): 350 Calories 6g Fat 10g Carbohydrates 42g Protein 842mg Sodium

Lamb with String Beans

Preparation Time : 10 minutes

Cooking Time : 1 hour

Servings : 6

Difficulty Level : Difficult

Ingredients:

- ¼ cup extra-virgin olive oil, divided
- 6 lamb chops, trimmed of extra fat
- 1 teaspoon sea salt, divided
- ½ teaspoon freshly ground black pepper
- 2 tablespoons tomato paste
- 1½ cups hot water
- 1-pound green beans, trimmed and halved crosswise
- 1 onion, chopped
- 2 tomatoes, chopped

Directions:

Cook 2 tablespoons of olive oil in large skillet until it shimmers. Season the lamb chops with ½ teaspoon of sea salt and 1/8 teaspoon of pepper. Cook the lamb in the hot oil for about 4 minutes per side until browned on both sides. Situate the meat to a platter and set aside.

Position the skillet back to the heat and put the remaining 2 tablespoons of olive oil. Heat until it shimmers.

In a bowl, melt the tomato paste in the hot water. Add it to the hot skillet along with the green beans, onion, tomatoes, and the remaining ½ teaspoon of sea salt and ¼ teaspoon of pepper. Bring to a simmer, using a spoon's side to scrape browned bits from the bottom of the pan.

Return the lamb chops to the pan. Allow to boil and adjust the heat to medium-low. Simmer for 45 minutes until the beans are soft, adding additional water as needed to adjust the sauce's thickness.

Nutrition (for 100g): 439 Calories 4g Fat 10g Carbohydrates 50g Protein 745mg Sodium

Chicken in Tomato-Balsamic Pan Sauce

Preparation Time : 10 minutes

Cooking Time : 20 minutes

Servings : 4

Difficulty Level : Average

Ingredients

- 2 (8 oz. or 226.7 g each) boneless chicken breasts, skinless
- ½ tsp. salt
- ½ tsp. ground pepper
- 3 tbsps. extra-virgin olive oil
- ½ c. halved cherry tomatoes
- 2 tbsps. sliced shallot
- ¼ c. balsamic vinegar
- 1 tbsp. minced garlic
- 1 tbsp. toasted fennel seeds, crushed
- 1 tbsp. butter

Directions:

Slice the chicken breasts into 4 pieces and beat them with a mallet till it reaches a thickness of a ¼ inch. Use ¼ teaspoons of pepper and salt to coat the chicken. Heat two tablespoons of oil in a skillet and keep the heat to a medium. Cook the chicken breasts on both sides for three minutes. Place it to a serving plate and cover it with foil to keep it warm.

Add one tablespoon oil, shallot, and tomatoes in a pan and cook till it softens. Add vinegar and boil the mix till the vinegar gets reduced by half. Put fennel seeds, garlic, salt, and pepper and cook for about four minutes. Pull it out from the heat and stir it with butter. Pour this sauce over chicken and serve.

Nutrition (for 100g): 294 Calories 17g Fat 10g Carbohydrates 2g Protein 639mg Sodium

Brown Rice, Feta, Fresh Pea, and Mint Salad

Preparation Time : 10 minutes

Cooking Time : 25 minutes

Servings : 4

Difficulty Level : Easy

Ingredients:

- 2 c. brown rice
- 3 c. water
- Salt
- 5 oz. or 141.7 g crumbled feta cheese
- 2 c. cooked peas
- ½ c. chopped mint, fresh
- 2 tbsps. olive oil
- Salt and pepper

Directions:

Place the brown rice, water, and salt into a saucepan over medium heat, cover, and bring to boiling point. Turn the lower heat and allow it to cook until the water has dissolved and the rice is soft but chewy. Leave to cool completely

Add the feta, peas, mint, olive oil, salt, and pepper to a salad bowl with the cooled rice and toss to combine Serve and enjoy!

Nutrition (for 100g): 613 Calories 18.2g Fat 45g Carbohydrates 12g Protein 755mg Sodium

Cauliflower Steaks with Olive Citrus Sauce

Preparation Time : 15 minutes

Cooking Time : 30 minutes

Servings : 4

Difficulty Level : Average

Ingredients:

- 1 or 2 large heads cauliflower
- 1/3 cup extra-virgin olive oil
- ¼ teaspoon kosher salt
- 1/8 teaspoon ground black pepper
- Juice of 1 orange
- Zest of 1 orange
- ¼ cup black olives, pitted and chopped
- 1 tablespoon Dijon or grainy mustard
- 1 tablespoon red wine vinegar
- ½ teaspoon ground coriander

Directions:

Preheat the oven to 400°F. Put parchment paper or foil into the baking sheet. Cut off the stem of the cauliflower so it will sit upright. Slice it vertically into four thick slabs. Place the cauliflower on the prepared baking sheet. Dash with the olive oil, salt, and black pepper. Bake for about 30 minutes.

In a medium bowl, stir the orange juice, orange zest, olives, mustard, vinegar, and coriander; mix well. Serve with the sauce.

Nutrition (for 100g): 265 Calories 21g Fat 4g Carbohydrates 5g Protein 693mg Sodium

Pistachio Mint Pesto Pasta

Preparation Time : 10 minutes

Cooking Time : 10 minutes

Servings : 4

Difficulty Level : Average

Ingredients:

- 8 ounces whole-wheat pasta
- 1 cup fresh mint
- ½ cup fresh basil
- 1/3 cup unsalted pistachios, shelled
- 1 garlic clove, peeled
- ½ teaspoon kosher salt
- Juice of ½ lime
- 1/3 cup extra-virgin olive oil

Directions:

Cook the pasta following the package directions. Drain, reserving ½ cup of the pasta water, and set aside. In a food processor, add the mint, basil, pistachios, garlic, salt, and lime juice. Process until the pistachios are coarsely ground. Stir in the olive oil in a slow, steady stream and process until incorporated.

In a large bowl, incorporate the pasta with the pistachio pesto. If a thinner, more saucy consistency is desired, add some of the reserved pasta water and toss well.

Nutrition (for 100g): 420 Calories3g Fat 2g Carbohydrates 11g Protein 593mg Sodium

Burst Cherry Tomato Sauce with Angel Hair Pasta

Preparation Time : 10 minutes

Cooking Time : 20 minutes

Servings : 4

Difficulty Level : Average

Ingredients:

- 8 ounces angel hair pasta
- 2 tablespoons extra-virgin olive oil
- 3 garlic cloves, minced
- 3 pints cherry tomatoes
- ½ teaspoon kosher salt
- ¼ teaspoon red pepper flakes
- ¾ cup fresh basil, chopped
- 1 tablespoon white balsamic vinegar (optional)
- ¼ cup grated Parmesan cheese (optional)

Directions:

Cook the pasta following the package directions. Drain and set aside.

Cook the olive oil in a skillet or large sauté pan over medium-high heat. Stir in the garlic and sauté for 30 seconds. Mix in the tomatoes, salt, and red pepper flakes and cook, stirring occasionally, until the tomatoes burst, about 15 minutes.

Take out from the heat and stir in the pasta and basil. Toss together well. (For out-of-season tomatoes, add the vinegar, if desired, and mix well.) Serve.

Nutrition (for 100g): 305 Calories 8g Fat 3g Carbohydrates 11g Protein 559mg Sodium

Baked Tofu with Sun-Dried Tomatoes and Artichokes

Preparation Time : 30 minutes

Cooking Time : 30 minutes

Servings : 4

Difficulty Level : Average

Ingredients:

- 1 (16-ounce) package extra-firm tofu, cut into 1-inch cubes
- 2 tablespoons extra-virgin olive oil, divided
- 2 tablespoons lemon juice, divided
- 1 tablespoon low-sodium soy sauce
- 1 onion, diced
- ½ teaspoon kosher salt
- 2 garlic cloves, minced
- 1 (14-ounce) can artichoke hearts, drained
- 8 sun-dried tomato
- ¼ teaspoon freshly ground black pepper
- 1 tablespoon white wine vinegar
- Zest of 1 lemon
- ¼ cup fresh parsley, chopped

Directions:

Prepare the oven to 400°F. Position the foil or parchment paper into the baking sheet. In a bowl, combine the tofu, 1 tablespoon of the olive oil, 1 tablespoon of the lemon juice, and the soy sauce. Set aside and marinate for 15 to 30 minutes. Arrange the tofu in a single layer on the prepared baking sheet and bake for 20 minutes, turning once, until light golden brown.

Cook the remaining 1 tablespoon olive oil in a large skillet or sauté pan over medium heat. Add the onion and salt; sauté until translucent, 5 to 6 minutes. Mix in the garlic and sauté for 30 seconds. Then put the artichoke hearts, sun-dried tomatoes, and black pepper and sauté for 5 minutes. Add the white wine vinegar and the remaining 1 tablespoon lemon juice and deglaze the pan, scraping up any brown bits. Take the pan from the heat and put in the lemon zest and parsley. Gently mix in the baked tofu.

Nutrition (for 100g): 230 Calories 14g Fat 5g Carbohydrates 14g Protein 593mg Sodium

Baked Mediterranean Tempeh with Tomatoes and Garlic

Preparation Time : 25 minutes, plus 4 hours to marinate

Cooking Time : 35 minutes

Servings : 4

Difficulty Level : Difficult

Ingredients:

- <u>For the Tempeh</u>
- 12 ounces tempeh
- ¼ cup white wine
- 2 tablespoons extra-virgin olive oil
- 2 tablespoons lemon juice
- Zest of 1 lemon
- ¼ teaspoon kosher salt
- ¼ teaspoon freshly ground black pepper
- <u>For the Tomatoes and Garlic Sauce</u>
- 1 tablespoon extra-virgin olive oil
- 1 onion, diced
- 3 garlic cloves, minced
- 1 (14.5-ounce) can no-salt-added crushed tomatoes
- 1 beefsteak tomato, diced
- 1 dried bay leaf
- 1 teaspoon white wine vinegar

- 1 teaspoon lemon juice
- 1 teaspoon dried oregano
- 1 teaspoon dried thyme
- ¾ teaspoon kosher salt
- ¼ cup basil, cut into ribbons

Directions:

To Make the Tempeh

Place the tempeh in a medium saucepan. Fill enough water to cover it by 1 to 2 inches. Bring to a boil over medium-high heat, cover, and lower heat to a simmer. Cook for 10 to 15 minutes. Remove the tempeh, pat dry, cool, and cut into 1-inch cubes.

Mix the white wine, olive oil, lemon juice, lemon zest, salt, and black pepper. Add the tempeh, cover the bowl, put in the refrigerator for 4 hours, or overnight. Preheat the oven to 375°F. Place the marinated tempeh and the marinade in a baking dish and cook for 15 minutes.

To Make the Tomatoes and Garlic Sauce

Cook the olive oil in a large skillet over medium heat. Add the onion and sauté until transparent, 3 to 5 minutes. Mix in the garlic and sauté for 30 seconds. Add the crushed tomatoes, beefsteak tomato, bay leaf, vinegar, lemon juice, oregano, thyme, and salt. Mix well. Simmer for 15 minutes.

Add the baked tempeh to the tomato mixture and gently mix together. Garnish with the basil.

SUBSTITUTION TIP: If you're out of tempeh or simply want to speed up the cooking process, you can swap in a 14.5-ounce can of white beans for the tempeh. Rinse the beans and put them to the sauce with the crushed tomatoes. It still makes a great vegan entrée in half the time!

Nutrition (for 100g): 330 Calories 20g Fat 4g Carbohydrates 18g Protein 693mg Sodium

Roasted Portobello Mushrooms with Kale and Red Onion

Preparation Time : 30 minutes

Cooking Time : 30 minutes

Servings : 4

Difficulty Level : Difficult

Ingredients:

- ¼ cup white wine vinegar
- 3 tablespoons extra-virgin olive oil, divided
- ½ teaspoon honey
- ¾ teaspoon kosher salt, divided
- ¼ teaspoon freshly ground black pepper
- 4 large portobello mushrooms, stems removed
- 1 red onion, julienned
- 2 garlic cloves, minced
- 1 (8-ounce) bunch kale, stemmed and chopped small
- ¼ teaspoon red pepper flakes
- ¼ cup grated Parmesan or Romano cheese

Directions:

Situate parchment paper or foil into the baking sheet. In a medium bowl, whisk together the vinegar, 1½ tablespoons of the olive oil, honey, ¼ teaspoon of the salt, and the black pepper. Lay the mushrooms on the baking sheet and pour the marinade over them. Marinate for 15 to 30 minutes.

Meanwhile, preheat the oven to 400°F. Bake the mushrooms for 20 minutes, turning over halfway through. Heat the remaining 1½ tablespoons olive oil in a large skillet or ovenproof sauté pan over medium-high heat. Add the onion and the remaining ½ teaspoon salt and sauté until golden brown, 5 to 6 minutes. Mix in the garlic and sauté for 30 seconds. Mix in the kale and red pepper flakes and sauté until the kale cooks down, about 5 minutes.

Remove the mushrooms from the oven and increase the temperature to broil. Carefully pour the liquid from the baking sheet into the pan with the kale mixture; mix well. Turn the mushrooms over so that the stem side is facing up. Spoon some of the kale mixture on top of each mushroom. Sprinkle 1 tablespoon Parmesan cheese on top of each. Broil until golden brown.

Nutrition (For 100g): 200 Calories 13g Fat 4g Carbohydrates 8g Protein

Balsamic Marinated Tofu with Basil and Oregano

Preparation Time : 40 minutes

Cooking Time : 30 minutes

Servings : 4

Difficulty Level : Average

Ingredients:

- ¼ cup extra-virgin olive oil
- ¼ cup balsamic vinegar
- 2 tablespoons low-sodium soy sauce
- 3 garlic cloves, grated
- 2 teaspoons pure maple syrup
- Zest of 1 lemon
- 1 teaspoon dried basil
- 1 teaspoon dried oregano
- ½ teaspoon dried thyme
- ½ teaspoon dried sage
- ¼ teaspoon kosher salt
- ¼ teaspoon freshly ground black pepper
- ¼ teaspoon red pepper flakes (optional)
- 1 (16-ounce) block extra firm tofu

Directions:

In a bowl or gallon zip-top bag, mix together the olive oil, vinegar, soy sauce, garlic, maple syrup, lemon zest, basil, oregano, thyme, sage, salt, black pepper, and red pepper flakes, if desired. Add the tofu and mix gently. Put in the refrigerator and marinate for 30 minutes, or up to overnight if you desire.

Prepare the oven to 425°F. Place parchment paper or foil into the baking sheet. Arrange the marinated tofu in a single layer on the prepared baking sheet. Bake for 20 to 30 minutes, flip over halfway through, until slightly crispy.

Nutrition (for 100g): 225 Calories 16g Fat 2g Carbohydrates 13g Protein 493mg Sodium

Ricotta, Basil, and Pistachio–Stuffed Zucchini

Preparation Time : 15 minutes

Cooking Time : 25 minutes

Servings : 4

Difficulty Level : Average

Ingredients:

- 2 medium zucchinis, halved lengthwise
- 1 tablespoon extra-virgin olive oil
- 1 onion, diced
- 1 teaspoon kosher salt
- 2 garlic cloves, minced
- ¾ cup ricotta cheese
- ¼ cup unsalted pistachios, shelled and chopped
- ¼ cup fresh basil, chopped
- 1 large egg, beaten
- ¼ teaspoon freshly ground black pepper

Directions:

Ready the oven to 425°F. Situate parchment paper or foil into the baking sheet. Scoop out the seeds/pulp from the zucchini, leaving ¼-inch flesh around the edges. Situate the pulp to a cutting board and chop off the pulp.

Cook the olive oil in a sauté pan over medium heat. Add the onion, pulp, and salt and sauté about 5 minutes. Add the garlic and sauté 30 seconds. Mix the ricotta cheese, pistachios, basil, egg, and black pepper. Add the onion mixture and mix well.

Place the 4 zucchini halves on the prepared baking sheet. Spread the zucchini halves with the ricotta mixture. Bake until golden brown.

Nutrition (for 100g): 200 Calories 12g Fat 3g Carbohydrates 11g Protein 836mg Sodium

Farro with Roasted Tomatoes and Mushrooms

Preparation Time : 20 minutes

Cooking Time : 1 hour

Servings : 4

Difficulty Level : Difficult

Ingredients:

- <u>For the Tomatoes</u>
- 2 pints cherry tomatoes
- 1 teaspoon extra-virgin olive oil
- ¼ teaspoon kosher salt
- <u>For the Farro</u>
- 3 to 4 cups water
- ½ cup farro
- ¼ teaspoon kosher salt
- <u>For the Mushrooms</u>
- 2 tablespoons extra-virgin olive oil
- 1 onion, julienned
- ½ teaspoon kosher salt
- ¼ teaspoon freshly ground black pepper
- 10 ounces baby bell mushrooms, stemmed and sliced thin
- ½ cup no-salt-added vegetable stock

- 1 (15-ounce) can low-sodium cannellini beans, drained and rinsed
- 1 cup baby spinach
- 2 tablespoons fresh basil, cut into ribbons
- ¼ cup pine nuts, toasted
- Aged balsamic vinegar (optional)

Directions:

To Make the Tomatoes

Preheat the oven to 400°F. Put parchment paper or foil into the baking sheet. Mix the tomatoes, olive oil, and salt together on the baking sheet and roast for 30 minutes.

To Make the Farro

Bring the water, farro, and salt to a boil in a medium saucepan or pot over high heat. Allow to simmer, and cook for 30 minutes, or until the farro is al dente. Drain and set aside.

To Make the Mushrooms

Cook the olive oil in a large skillet or sauté pan over medium-low heat. Add the onions, salt, and black pepper and sauté until golden brown and starting to caramelize, about 15 minutes. Stir in the mushrooms, increase the heat to medium, and sauté until the liquid has evaporated and the mushrooms brown, about 10 minutes. Stir in the vegetable stock and deglaze the pan, scraping up any brown bits, and reduce the liquid for about 5 minutes. Add the beans and warm through, about 3 minutes.

Remove and stir in the spinach, basil, pine nuts, roasted tomatoes, and farro. Dash with balsamic vinegar, if desired.

Nutrition (for 100g): 375 Calories 15g Fat 10g Carbohydrates 14g Protein 769mg Sodium

Baked Orzo with Eggplant, Swiss Chard, and Mozzarella

Preparation Time : 20 minutes

Cooking Time : 60 minutes

Servings : 4

Difficulty Level : Average

Ingredients:

- 2 tablespoons extra-virgin olive oil
- 1 large (1-pound) eggplant, diced small
- 2 carrots, peeled and diced small
- 2 celery stalks, diced small
- 1 onion, diced small
- ½ teaspoon kosher salt
- 3 garlic cloves, minced
- ¼ teaspoon freshly ground black pepper
- 1 cup whole-wheat orzo
- 1 teaspoon no-salt-added tomato paste
- 1½ cups no-salt-added vegetable stock
- 1 cup Swiss chard, stemmed and chopped small
- 2 tablespoons fresh oregano, chopped
- Zest of 1 lemon
- 4 ounces mozzarella cheese, diced small
- ¼ cup grated Parmesan cheese
- 2 tomatoes, sliced ½-inch-thick

Directions:

Preheat the oven to 400°F. Cook the olive oil in a large oven-safe sauté pan over medium heat. Add the eggplant, carrots, celery, onion, and salt and sauté about 10 minutes. Add the garlic and black pepper and sauté about 30 seconds. Add the orzo and tomato paste and sauté 1 minute. Mix in the vegetable stock and deglaze the pan, scraping up the brown bits. Add the Swiss chard, oregano, and lemon zest and stir until the chard wilts.

Pull out and put in the mozzarella cheese. Smooth the top of the orzo mixture flat. Sprinkle the Parmesan cheese over the top. Spread the tomatoes in a single layer on top of the Parmesan cheese. Bake for 45 minutes.

Nutrition (for 100g): 470 Calories 17g Fat 7g Carbohydrates 18g Protein 769mg Sodium

Barley Risotto with Tomatoes

Preparation Time : 20 minutes

Cooking Time : 45 minutes

Servings : 4

Difficulty Level : Average

Ingredients:

- 2 tablespoons extra-virgin olive oil
- 2 celery stalks, diced
- ½ cup shallots, diced
- 4 garlic cloves, minced
- 3 cups no-salt-added vegetable stock
- 1 (14.5-ounce) can no-salt-added diced tomatoes
- 1 (14.5-ounce) can no-salt-added crushed tomatoes
- 1 cup pearl barley
- Zest of 1 lemon
- 1 teaspoon kosher salt
- ½ teaspoon smoked paprika
- ¼ teaspoon red pepper flakes
- ¼ teaspoon freshly ground black pepper
- 4 thyme sprigs
- 1 dried bay leaf
- 2 cups baby spinach
- ½ cup crumbled feta cheese
- 1 tablespoon fresh oregano, chopped

- 1 tablespoon fennel seeds, toasted (optional)

Directions:

Cook the olive oil in a large saucepan over medium heat. Add the celery and shallots and sauté, about 4 to 5 minutes. Add the garlic and sauté 30 seconds. Add the vegetable stock, diced tomatoes, crushed tomatoes, barley, lemon zest, salt, paprika, red pepper flakes, black pepper, thyme, and the bay leaf, and mix well. Let it boil, then lower to low, and simmer. Cook, stirring occasionally, for 40 minutes.

Remove the bay leaf and thyme sprigs. Stir in the spinach. In a small bowl, combine the feta, oregano, and fennel seeds. Serve the barley risotto in bowls topped with the feta mixture.

Nutrition (for 100g): 375 Calories 12g Fat 13g Carbohydrates 11g Protein 799mg Sodium

Chickpeas and Kale with Spicy Pomodoro Sauce

Preparation Time : 10 minutes

Cooking Time : 35 minutes

Servings : 4

Difficulty Level : Easy

Ingredients:

- 2 tablespoons extra-virgin olive oil
- 4 garlic cloves, sliced
- 1 teaspoon red pepper flakes
- 1 (28-ounce) can no-salt-added crushed tomatoes
- 1 teaspoon kosher salt
- ½ teaspoon honey
- 1 bunch kale, stemmed and chopped
- 2 (15-ounce) cans low-sodium chickpeas, drained and rinsed
- ¼ cup fresh basil, chopped
- ¼ cup grated pecorino Romano cheese

Directions:

Cook the olive oil in a sauté pan over medium heat. Stir in the garlic and red pepper flakes and sauté until the garlic is a light golden brown, about 2 minutes. Add the tomatoes, salt, and honey and mix well. Reduce the heat to low and simmer for 20 minutes.

Add the kale and mix in well. Cook about 5 minutes. Add the chickpeas and simmer about 5 minutes. Remove from heat and stir in the basil. Serve topped with pecorino cheese.

Nutrition (for 100g): 420 Calories 13g Fat 12g Carbohydrates 20g Protein 882mg Sodium

Roasted Feta with Kale and Lemon Yogurt

Preparation Time : 15 minutes

Cooking Time : 20 minutes

Servings : 4

Difficulty Level : Average

Ingredients:

- 1 tablespoon extra-virgin olive oil
- 1 onion, julienned
- ¼ teaspoon kosher salt
- 1 teaspoon ground turmeric
- ½ teaspoon ground cumin
- ½ teaspoon ground coriander
- ¼ teaspoon freshly ground black pepper
- 1 bunch kale, stemmed and chopped
- 7-ounce block feta cheese, cut into ¼-inch-thick slices
- ½ cup plain Greek yogurt
- 1 tablespoon lemon juice

Directions:

Preheat the oven to 400°F. Fry the olive oil in a large ovenproof skillet or sauté pan over medium heat. Add the onion and salt; sauté until lightly golden brown, about 5 minutes. Add the turmeric, cumin, coriander, and black pepper; sauté for 30 seconds. Add the kale and sauté about 2 minutes. Add ½ cup water and continue to cook down the kale, about 3 minutes.

Remove from the heat and place the feta cheese slices on top of the kale mixture. Introduce in the oven and bake until the feta softens, 10 to 12 minutes. In a small bowl, combine the yogurt and lemon juice. Serve the kale and feta cheese topped with the lemon yogurt.

Nutrition (for 100g): 210 Calories 14g Fat 2g Carbohydrates 11g Protein 836mg Sodium

Roasted Eggplant and Chickpeas with Tomato Sauce

Preparation Time : 15 minutes

Cooking Time : 60 minutes

Servings : 4

Difficulty Level : Difficult

Ingredients:

- Olive oil cooking spray
- 1 large (about 1 pound) eggplant, sliced into ¼-inch-thick rounds
- 1 teaspoon kosher salt, divided
- 1 tablespoon extra-virgin olive oil
- 3 garlic cloves, minced
- 1 (28-ounce) can no-salt-added crushed tomatoes
- ½ teaspoon honey
- ¼ teaspoon freshly ground black pepper
- 2 tablespoons fresh basil, chopped
- 1 (15-ounce) can no-salt-added or low-sodium chickpeas, drained and rinsed
- ¾ cup crumbled feta cheese
- 1 tablespoon fresh oregano, chopped

Directions:

Preheat the oven to 425°F. Grease and line two baking sheets with foil and lightly spray with olive oil cooking spray. Spread the eggplant in a single layer and sprinkle with ½ teaspoon of the salt. Bake for 20 minutes, turning once halfway, until lightly golden brown.

Meanwhile, heat the olive oil in a large saucepan over medium heat. Mix in the garlic and sauté for 30 seconds. Add the crushed tomatoes, honey, the remaining ½ teaspoon salt, and black pepper. Simmer about 20 minutes, until the sauce reduces a bit and thickens. Stir in the basil.

After removing the eggplant from the oven, reduce the oven temperature to 375°F. In a large rectangular or oval baking dish, spoon in the chickpeas and 1 cup sauce. Layer the eggplant slices on top, overlapping as necessary to cover the chickpeas. Lay the remaining sauce on top of the eggplant. Sprinkle the feta cheese and oregano on top.

Wrap the baking dish with foil and bake for 15 minutes. Pull out the foil and bake an additional 15 minutes.

Nutrition (for 100g): 320 Calories 11g Fat 12g Carbohydrates 14g Protein 773mg Sodium

Baked Falafel Sliders

Preparation Time : 10 minutes

Cooking Time : 30 minutes

Servings : 6

Difficulty Level : Average

Ingredients:

- Olive oil cooking spray
- 1 (15-ounce) can low-sodium chickpeas, drained and rinsed
- 1 onion, roughly chopped
- 2 garlic cloves, peeled
- 2 tablespoons fresh parsley, chopped
- 2 tablespoons whole-wheat flour
- ½ teaspoon ground coriander
- ½ teaspoon ground cumin
- ½ teaspoon baking powder
- ½ teaspoon kosher salt
- ¼ teaspoon freshly ground black pepper

Directions:

Preheat the oven to 350°F. Put parchment paper or foil and lightly spray with olive oil cooking spray in the baking sheet.

In a food processor, mix in the chickpeas, onion, garlic, parsley, flour, coriander, cumin, baking powder, salt, and black pepper. Blend until smooth.

Make 6 slider patties, each with a heaping ¼ cup of mixture, and arrange on the prepared baking sheet. Bake for 30 minutes. Serve.

Nutrition (for 100g): 90 Calories 1g Fat 3g Carbohydrates 4g Protein 803mg Sodium

Portobello Caprese

Preparation Time : 15 minutes

Cooking Time : 30 minutes

Servings : 2

Difficulty Level : Difficult

Ingredients:

- 1 tablespoon olive oil
- 1 cup cherry tomatoes
- Salt and black pepper, to taste
- 4 large fresh basil leaves, thinly sliced, divided
- 3 medium garlic cloves, minced
- 2 large portobello mushrooms, stems removed
- 4 pieces mini Mozzarella balls
- 1 tablespoon Parmesan cheese, grated

Directions:

Prepare the oven to 350°F (180ºC). Grease a baking pan with olive oil. Drizzle 1 tablespoon olive oil in a nonstick skillet, and heat over medium-high heat. Add the tomatoes to the skillet, and sprinkle salt and black pepper to season. Prick some holes on the tomatoes for juice during the cooking. Put the lid on and cook the tomatoes for 10 minutes or until tender.

Reserve 2 teaspoons of basil and add the remaining basil and garlic to the skillet. Crush the tomatoes with a spatula, then cook for half a minute. Stir constantly during the cooking. Set aside. Arrange the mushrooms in the baking pan, cap side down, and sprinkle with salt and black pepper to taste.

Spoon the tomato mixture and Mozzarella balls on the gill of the mushrooms, then scatter with Parmesan cheese to coat well. Bake until the mushrooms are fork-tender and the cheeses are browned. Pull out the stuffed mushrooms from the oven and serve with basil on top.

Nutrition (for 100g): 285 Calories 21.8g Fat 2.1g Carbohydrates 14.3g Protein 823mg Sodium

Mushroom and Cheese Stuffed Tomatoes

Preparation Time : 15 minutes

Cooking Time : 20 minutes

Servings : 4

Difficulty Level : Average

Ingredients:

- 4 large ripe tomatoes
- 1 tablespoon olive oil
- ½ pound (454 g) white or cremini mushrooms, sliced
- 1 tablespoon fresh basil, chopped
- ½ cup yellow onion, diced
- 1 tablespoon fresh oregano, chopped
- 2 garlic cloves, minced
- ½ teaspoon salt
- ¼ teaspoon freshly ground black pepper
- 1 cup part-skim Mozzarella cheese, shredded
- 1 tablespoon Parmesan cheese, grated

Directions:

Ready the oven to 375°F (190ºC). Cut a ½-inch slice off the top of each tomato. Scoop the pulp into a bowl and leave ½-inch tomato shells. Arrange the tomatoes on a baking sheet lined with aluminum foil. Heat the olive oil in a nonstick skillet over medium heat.

Add the mushrooms, basil, onion, oregano, garlic, salt, and black pepper to the skillet and sauté for 5 minutes.

Pour the mixture to the tomato pulp bowl, then add the Mozzarella cheese and stir to combine well. Spoon the mixture into each tomato shell, then top with a layer of Parmesan. Bake in the preheated oven for 15 minutes or until the cheese is bubbly and the tomatoes are soft. Pull out the stuffed tomatoes from the oven and serve warm.

Nutrition (for 100g): 254 Calories 14.7g Fat 5.2g Carbohydrates 17.5g Protein 783mg Sodium

Tabbouleh

Preparation Time : 15 minutes

Cooking Time : 5 minutes

Servings : 6

Difficulty Level : Average

Ingredients:

- 4 tablespoons olive oil, divided
- 4 cups riced cauliflower
- 3 garlic cloves, finely minced
- Salt and black pepper, to taste
- ½ large cucumber, peeled, seeded, and chopped
- ½ cup Italian parsley, chopped
- Juice of 1 lemon
- 2 tablespoons minced red onion
- ½ cup mint leaves, chopped
- ½ cup pitted Kalamata olives, chopped
- 1 cup cherry tomatoes, quartered
- 2 cups baby arugula or spinach leaves
- 2 medium avocados, peeled, pitted, and diced

Directions:

Warm 2 tablespoons olive oil in a nonstick skillet over medium-high heat. Add the rice cauliflower, garlic, salt, and black pepper to the skillet and sauté for 3 minutes or until fragrant. Transfer them to a large bowl.

Add the cucumber, parsley, lemon juice, red onion, mint, olives, and remaining olive oil to the bowl. Toss to combine well. Reserve the bowl in the refrigerator for at least 30 minutes.

Remove the bowl from the refrigerator. Add the cherry tomatoes, arugula, avocado to the bowl. Season well, and toss to combine well. Serve chilled.

Nutrition (for 100g): 198 Calories 17.5g Fat 6.2g Carbohydrates 4.2g Protein 773mg Sodium

Spicy Broccoli Rabe And Artichoke Hearts

Preparation Time : 5 minutes

Cooking Time : 15 minutes

Servings : 4

Difficulty Level : Average

Ingredients:

- 3 tablespoons olive oil, divided
- 2 pounds (907 g) fresh broccoli rabe
- 3 garlic cloves, finely minced
- 1 teaspoon red pepper flakes
- 1 teaspoon salt, plus more to taste
- 13.5 ounces (383 g) artichoke hearts
- 1 tablespoon water
- 2 tablespoons red wine vinegar
- Freshly ground black pepper, to taste

Directions:

Warm 2 tablespoons olive oil in a nonstick skillet over medium-high skillet. Add the broccoli, garlic, red pepper flakes, and salt to the skillet and sauté for 5 minutes or until the broccoli is soft.

Put the artichoke hearts to the skillet and sauté for 2 more minutes or until tender. Add water to the skillet and turn down the heat to low. Put the lid on and simmer for 5 minutes. Meanwhile, combine the vinegar and 1 tablespoon of olive oil in a bowl.

Drizzle the simmered broccoli and artichokes with oiled vinegar, and sprinkle with salt and black pepper. Toss to combine well before serving.

Nutrition (for 100g): 272 Calories 21.5g Fat 9.8g Carbohydrates 11.2g Protein 736mg Sodium

Shakshuka

Preparation Time : 10 minutes

Cooking Time : 25 minutes

Servings : 4

Difficulty Level : Difficult

Ingredients:

- 5 tablespoons olive oil, divided
- 1 red bell pepper, finely diced
- ½ small yellow onion, finely diced
- 14 ounces (397 g) crushed tomatoes, with juices
- 6 ounces (170 g) frozen spinach, thawed and drained of excess liquid
- 1 teaspoon smoked paprika
- 2 garlic cloves, finely minced
- 2 teaspoons red pepper flakes
- 1 tablespoon capers, roughly chopped
- 1 tablespoon water
- 6 large eggs
- ¼ teaspoon freshly ground black pepper
- ¾ cup feta or goat cheese, crumbled
- ¼ cup fresh flat-leaf parsley or cilantro, chopped

Directions:

Ready the oven to 300ºF (150ºC). Heat 2 tablespoons olive oil in an oven-safe skillet over medium-high heat. Sauté the bell pepper and onion to the skillet until the onion is translucent and the bell pepper is soft.

Add the tomatoes and juices, spinach, paprika, garlic, red pepper flakes, capers, water, and 2 tablespoons olive oil to the skillet. Stir well and bring to a boil. Set down the heat to low, then put the lid on and simmer for 5 minutes.

Crack the eggs over the sauce, keep a little space between each egg, leave the egg intact and sprinkle with freshly ground black pepper. Cook until the eggs reach the right doneness.

Scatter the cheese over the eggs and sauce, and bake in the preheated oven for 5 minutes or until the cheese is frothy and golden brown. Drizzle with the remaining 1 tablespoon olive oil and spread the parsley on top before serving warm.

Nutrition (for 100g): 335 Calories 26.5g Fat 5g Carbohydrates 16.8g Protein 736mg Sodium

Spanakopita

Preparation Time : 15 minutes

Cooking Time : 50 minutes

Servings : 6

Difficulty Level : Difficult

Ingredients:

- 6 tablespoons olive oil, divided
- 1 small yellow onion, diced
- 4 cups frozen chopped spinach
- 4 garlic cloves, minced
- ½ teaspoon salt
- ½ teaspoon freshly ground black pepper
- 4 large eggs, beaten
- 1 cup ricotta cheese
- ¾ cup feta cheese, crumbled
- ¼ cup pine nuts

Directions:

Grease baking dish with 2 tablespoons olive oil. Organize the oven at 375 degrees F. Heat 2 tablespoons olive oil in a nonstick skillet over medium-high heat. Mix in the onion to the skillet and sauté for 6 minutes or until translucent and tender.

Add the spinach, garlic, salt, and black pepper to the skillet and sauté for 5 minutes more. Place them to a bowl and set aside.

Combine the beaten eggs and ricotta cheese in a separate bowl, then pour them in to the bowl of spinach mixture. Stir to mix well.

Fill the mixture into the baking dish, and tilt the dish so the mixture coats the bottom evenly. Bake until it begins to set. Take out the baking dish from the oven, and spread the feta cheese and pine nuts on top, then dash with remaining 2 tablespoons olive oil.

Return the baking dish to the oven and bake for another 15 minutes or until the top is golden brown. Remove the dish from the oven. Allow the spanakopita to cool for a few minutes and slice to serve.

Nutrition (for 100g): 340 Calories 27.3g Fat 10.1g Carbohydrates 18.2g Protein 781mg Sodium

Ratatouille

Preparation Time : 15 minutes

Cooking Time : 7 hours

Servings : 6

Difficulty Level : Average

Ingredients:

- 3 tablespoons extra-virgin olive oil
- 1 large eggplant, unpeeled, sliced
- 2 large onions, sliced
- 4 small zucchinis, sliced
- 2 green bell peppers
- 6 large tomatoes, cut in ½-inch wedges
- 2 tablespoons fresh flat-leaf parsley, chopped
- 1 teaspoon dried basil
- 2 garlic cloves, minced
- 2 teaspoons sea salt
- ¼ teaspoon freshly ground black pepper

Direction:

Fill the insert of the slow cooker with 2 tablespoons olive oil. Arrange the vegetables slices, strips, and wedges alternately in the insert of the slow cooker. Spread the parsley on top of the vegetables, and season with basil, garlic, salt, and black pepper. Drizzle with the remaining olive oil. Close and cook on LOW for 7 hours until the vegetables are tender. Transfer the vegetables on a plate and serve warm.

Nutrition (for 100g): 265 Calories 1.7g Fat 13.7g Carbohydrates 8.3g Protein 800mg Sodium

Gemista

Preparation Time : 15 minutes

Cooking Time : 4 hours

Servings : 4

Difficulty Level : Average

Ingredients:

- 2 tablespoons extra-virgin olive oil
- 4 large bell peppers, any color
- ½ cup uncooked couscous
- 1 teaspoon oregano
- 1 garlic clove, minced
- 1 cup crumbled feta cheese
- 1 (15-ounce / 425-g) can cannellini beans, rinsed and drained
- Salt and pepper, to taste
- 1 lemon wedges
- 4 green onions, white and green parts separated, thinly sliced

Direction:

Cut a ½-inch slice below the stem from the top of the bell pepper. Discard the stem only and chop the sliced top portion under the stem, and reserve in a bowl. Hollow the bell pepper with a spoon. Grease the slow cooker with oil.

Incorporate the remaining ingredients, except for the green parts of the green onion and lemon wedges, to the bowl of chopped bell pepper top. Stir to mix well. Spoon the mixture in the hollowed bell pepper, and arrange the stuffed bell peppers in the slow cooker, then drizzle with more olive oil.

Seal the slow cooker lid on and cook on HIGH for 4 hours or until the bell peppers are soft.

Remove the bell peppers from the slow cooker and serve on a plate. Sprinkle with green parts of the green onions, and squeeze the lemon wedges on top before serving.

Nutrition (for 100g): 246 Calories 9g Fat 6.5g Carbohydrates 11.1g Protein 698mg Sodium

Stuffed Cabbage Rolls

Preparation Time : 15 minutes

Cooking Time : 2 hours

Servings : 4

Difficulty Level : Difficult

Ingredients:

- 4 tablespoons olive oil, divided
- 1 large head green cabbage, cored
- 1 large yellow onion, chopped
- 3 ounces (85 g) feta cheese, crumbled
- ½ cup dried currants
- 3 cups cooked pearl barley
- 2 tablespoons fresh flat-leaf parsley, chopped
- 2 tablespoons pine nuts, toasted
- ½ teaspoon sea salt
- ½ teaspoon black pepper
- 15 ounces (425 g) crushed tomatoes, with the juice
- 1 tablespoon apple cider vinegar
- ½ cup apple juice

Directions:

Brush off the insert of the slow cooker with 2 tablespoons olive oil. Blanch the cabbage in a pot of water for 8 minutes. Take it from the water, and set aside, then separate 16 leaves from the cabbage. Set aside.

Drizzle the remaining olive oil in a nonstick skillet, and heat over medium heat. Stir in the onion to the skillet and cook until the onion and bell pepper is tender. Transfer the onion to a bowl.

Add the feta cheese, currants, barley, parsley, and pine nuts to the bowl of cooked onion, then sprinkle with ¼ teaspoon of salt and ¼ teaspoon of black pepper.

Arrange the cabbage leaves on a clean work surface. Scoop 1/3 cup of the mixture on the center of each plate, then fold the edge onto the mixture and roll it up. Place the cabbage rolls in the slow cooker, seam side down.

Incorporate the remaining ingredients in a separate bowl, then pour the mixture over the cabbage rolls. Seal slow cooker lid on and cook on HIGH for 2 hours. Remove the cabbage rolls from the slow cooker and serve warm.

Nutrition (for 100g): 383 Calories 14.7g Fat 12.9g Carbohydrates 10.7g Protein 838mg Sodium

Lightning Source UK Ltd.
Milton Keynes UK
UKHW020644130521
383655UK00010B/453